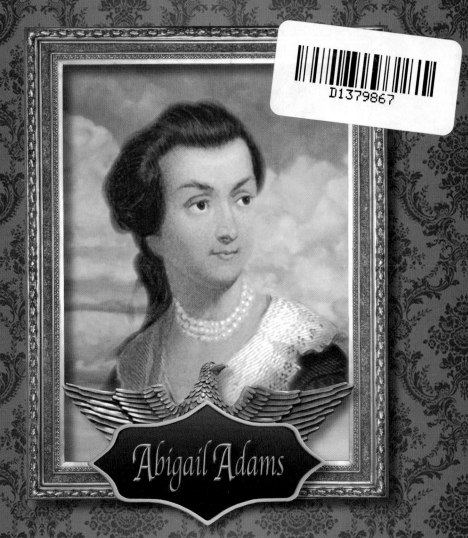

Abigail Adams

by PeggySue Wells

FIRST LADIES ⫽ SECOND TO NONE

PURPLE TOAD
PUBLISHING

FIRST LADIES SECOND TO NONE

Abigail Adams
Dolley Madison
Edith Wilson
Eleanor Roosevelt
Hillary Rodham Clinton
Mary Todd Lincoln

PUBLISHER'S NOTE: The data in this book has been researched in depth, and to the best of our knowledge is factual. Although every measure is taken to give an accurate account, Purple Toad Publishing makes no warranty of the accuracy of the information and is not liable for damages caused by inaccuracies.

Unless otherwise noted, the stories herein contain fictional conversation based on what historical documents suggest might have been said.

Printing   1   2   3   4   5   6   7   8   9

Publisher's Cataloging-in-Publication Data
Wells, PeggySue.
   Abigail Adams / written by PeggySue Wells.
      p. cm.
            Includes bibliographic references and index.
            ISBN 9781624691782
1. Adams, Abigail, 1744-1818—Juvenile literature.
2. Adams, John, 1735-1826—Juvenile literature. 3.
Presidents' spouses—United States—Biography—
Juvenile literature. I. Series: First Ladies : Second to None.
   E322.1.A38 2016
   973.44092
         Library of Congress Control Number: 2015941824
eBook ISBN: 9781624691799

Contents

Chapter One
DAME SCHOOL

"If you complain of neglect of Education in sons, What shall I say with regard to daughters, who every day experience the want of it. . . . If we mean to have Heroes, Statesmen and Philosophers, we should have learned women."[1]

To John Adams August 14, 1776

From Abigail Adams

"Papa, I want to go to school, too." Abigail was watching her younger brother, William, getting ready for school. "It's not fair that only boys get to learn."

The Reverend William Smith came to stand next to his daughter. "You learn to read in dame school at home. And to write and cipher."

She shrugged. "Just enough to be a wife and run a home."

"There is much to the operation of household and family, Abigail." He placed a hand on her slight shoulder. "You know a great deal about herbs for medicines and are a comfort when you and your mother visit the sick and elderly."

"I want to know as much as you, Papa." She thought of the long Sunday mornings when he preached to the members of their Congregational church. "Why shouldn't girls learn as much as boys?"

As a girl in Colonial Massachusetts, Abigail was an eager learner. She continued to read books on all topics long after her formal education was over.

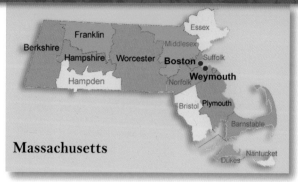

Massachusetts

Pastor Smith sighed. While sending girls to school wasn't customary, Abigail knew he would find a way to teach her. Wasting a mind as sharp as Abigail's, he had told her, reminded him of the Bible Story of the unwise steward. He buried the coin he was given instead of investing it and letting the money grow. Her father led her into his library and pointed to the shelves of books. "In these pages are Latin, religion, philosophy, poetry, and the world that lies beyond our city of Weymouth." He opened a book of detailed maps. "Let's begin your education with these, shall we?"

Instructed by her father, Abigail absorbed the contents of their library. In addition to mathematics and economics, she studied classic works of great authors, including John Milton and William Shakespeare. But the subject she liked the most was politics. Who should govern groups of peoples? How should communities be governed?

Occasionally, friends of the Smiths warned Abigail's father about allowing his daughter to learn too much. In an age when women were not allowed to vote, and were discouraged from talking about government and economics, these men preferred wives who did not think on their own.

Abigail's father did not see things their way. And he need not have worried. When a young lawyer named John Adams met 17-year-old Abigail, it was her mind that he admired. Soon John found ways to pass south of Boston through the Smiths' small town of Weymouth. He would visit her, and they would also write letters to one another. Their letters would number more than 1,100 and become one of America's greatest legacies.

Family Roots

On November 11, 1744, William Smith and Elizabeth Quincy Smith welcomed their second daughter, Abigail. Built in Weymouth, Massachusetts,

Abigail Adams' childhood home

in 1685, the Smith home was nearly 60 years old when Abigail was born there, and she lived at that address until she was nearly 20 years old. Abigail's sister, Mary, was three years old when Abigail joined the household. Later, siblings William and Betsy completed the family. Abigail was a small baby who experienced bouts of illness throughout her life.

Abigail's father was the minister at the Weymouth Congregational Church. William's father and grandfather were also ministers. Abigail's mother was a member of the prominent Quincy family. Elizabeth's father had served more than two decades in the House of Representatives and on the Supreme Court. Throughout the Massachusetts Bay Colony, the Smith and Quincy families were highly regarded. Traced back over six centuries, Abigail's ancestry included English and Welsh, as well as connections to royal lines in Belgium, France, Germany, Holland, Hungary, Ireland, Italy, Spain, and Switzerland.[2]

Like most households in colonial Massachusetts, the Smith family produced their own food by gardening, raising farm animals, fishing, and hunting. Meat was salted and smoked to preserve it through the northeastern winters. Clothes were washed by hand with lye soap, which Abigail learned to make from the ashes of hearth fires. Laundry was hung to dry and pressed with an iron heated on the stove.

Intelligent and Opinionated

When grown, Abigail was five feet one inch tall with brown eyes and brown hair. In the summer of 1762, her sister, Mary, married Richard Cranch. Richard had brought his friend and fellow Harvard graduate, John Adams,

John Adams

to meet the Smiths in 1759. At first, neither John nor Abigail had been impressed with each other, but that soon changed. Two years later, John was an attorney and had inherited property in Braintree from his father. He divided his time between farming and growing his law business.

Both John and Abigail were well read. They talked about politics, literature, and many other things. The couple gave each other nicknames in their letters. John was Abigail's Spartan general Lysander. She was his Diana, goddess of purity, or Portia of Shakespeare's *Merchant of Venice,* who was famed for her legal skills. He also called her Miss Adorable. Throughout their lives together, Abigail and John often addressed letters to each other as "My dearest friend."[3] After their marriage, Abigail referred to John as "the tenderest of husbands," and her "good man."

After an extended courtship, Abigail married John Adams on October 25, 1764, in a ceremony conducted by her father. Abigail was not quite 20 years old, and John was ten years her senior.

The newlyweds settled into John's family house in Braintree. On their "sweet little farm" one mile from the sea at the foot of Penn's Hill, Abigail ran the kitchen, milked cows, collected eggs from chickens, tended the garden, and made clothes. She and John shared deep affections for family, farm, books, and writing letters. Lifelong learners, they read books and engaged in intellectual conversations. The two were devout Christians and independent thinkers.[4]

On July 14, 1765, the couple welcomed their first child, Abigail Smith Adams, whom they called Nabby. Despite the calm rural setting where she was born, Nabby arrived in the midst of rising political conflict that promised to change the world. [5]

Colonial Girls

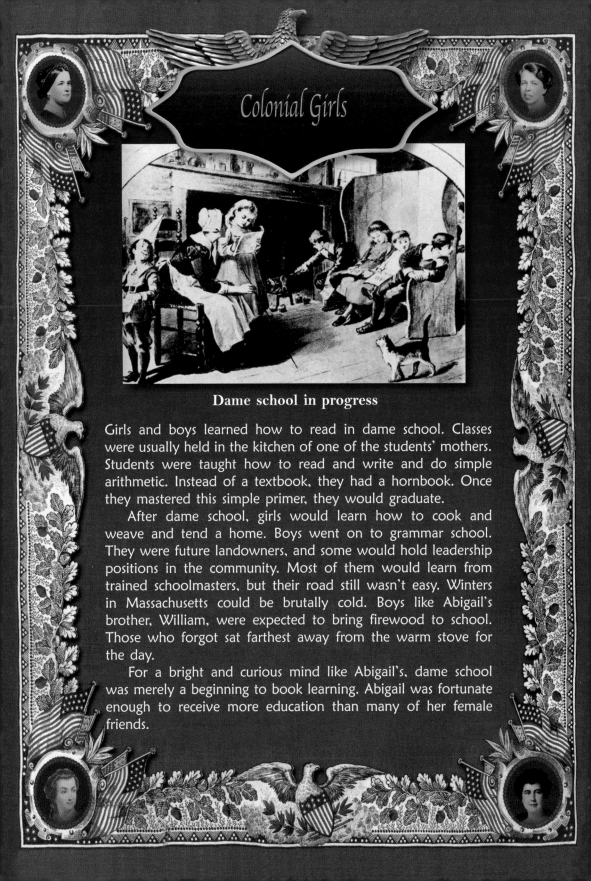

Dame school in progress

Girls and boys learned how to read in dame school. Classes were usually held in the kitchen of one of the students' mothers. Students were taught how to read and write and do simple arithmetic. Instead of a textbook, they had a hornbook. Once they mastered this simple primer, they would graduate.

After dame school, girls would learn how to cook and weave and tend a home. Boys went on to grammar school. They were future landowners, and some would hold leadership positions in the community. Most of them would learn from trained schoolmasters, but their road still wasn't easy. Winters in Massachusetts could be brutally cold. Boys like Abigail's brother, William, were expected to bring firewood to school. Those who forgot sat farthest away from the warm stove for the day.

For a bright and curious mind like Abigail's, dame school was merely a beginning to book learning. Abigail was fortunate enough to receive more education than many of her female friends.

Chapter Two
TAXES AND TENSION

"We live, my dear soul, in an age of trial. What will be the consequence, I know not."[1]

John Adams to Abigail, 1774

"Tensions between the colonists and Great Britain are mounting," John said when he arrived home, and kissed Abigail's cheek.

While her husband tried cases in Boston, Plymouth, Salem, and Worcester, Abigail remained in Braintree, later renamed Quincy, to run the farm. "Have our boycotts of European goods changed Parliament's decision? Doing without china, crystal, and perfume is not difficult, but I miss sugar and fine fabric."

John lifted baby Nabby from Abigail's arms and was rewarded with a smile from his firstborn. "Parliament retaliated with the Stamp Act. Every printed item is taxed, from almanacs and books to playing cards, licenses, newspapers, and pamphlets."

Abigail sat down to absorb this information. "Does that include contracts, deeds, and wills in your law practice?"

From New Hampshire to South Carolina, colonists protested the Stamp Act with riots and political cartoons. Fearful stamp distributors in the 13 colonies resigned and Parliament repealed the Stamp Act.

"Even bills I prepare for my legal clients."

Abigail glanced around the neat room. John's office was part of the lean-to added on to their saltbox home. "This tax affects everything you do. It's unfair that we don't have a voice among the lawmakers."

"Our communities are divided," John said. "Loyalists remain loyal to the crown. Patriots proclaim, 'No taxation without representation.'"

Through the window Abigail saw the apple orchard and land she farmed during John's absences. The work around their homestead was never-ending, and now she had Nabby to care for. Still, Abigail knew her husband was the right man to find solutions in these turbulent times. "What will you do?"

With Nabby happily in his arms, John sat next to Abigail. "The town council meets next week. I know I just arrived home, but I must be at that meeting to get these taxes repealed."

Abigail nodded.

"Write to me," he said. "I value your insights."

She looked at her ink-stained fingers. "As always." Despite the miles that separated the couple, writing letters kept them connected.

The heavy taxes were England's response to the recent war. From 1754 to 1763, the British had defended their American colonies during the French and Indian War. The victory had gone to Great Britain, along with the great expense of

Map of the 13 Colonies

Lake Huron

Lake Michigan

Lake Ontario

Lake Erie

Saint Lawrence River

Montreal

Massachusetts (Maine Province)

New Hampshire

Massachusetts

New York

Rhode Island

Connecticut

Pennsylvania

New Jersey

Delaware

Maryland

Virginia

Appalachian Mountains

North Carolina

Southern Carolina

Georgia

Atlantic Ocean

Gulf of Mexico

1 - Boston
2 - New York
3 - Philadelphie
4 - Baltimore
5 - Richmond
6 - Charlestown
7 - Savannah

fighting. Since the battle had been fought in the colonies, the British government decided the colonists should refill the British treasury.

Though the colonists, including Abigail and John, were English citizens, they were not given a voice in the decision when Great Britain levied taxes. One of these taxes, the Molasses Act of 1733, charged businessmen to import molasses. Merchants responded by boycotting European goods and merchandise including furniture, soap, tea, and wine.

Doing without products from Europe was inconvenient, but the Stamp Act of 1765 affected everyone. Next, the Quartering Act required colonists to house British soldiers. Expressing the political beliefs he and Abigail had discussed for years, John penned *A Dissertation on the Canon and the Feudal Law*. In it, he declared that American freedoms were rights established by British law and the sacrifice of generations of Americans. The piece was hailed by Ezra Stiles, clergyman and the future president of Yale University, as "one of the best that has been written."[2]

General Johnson Saving a Wounded French Officer from the Tomahawk of a North American Indian **shows Native American, British, and French soldiers from the French and Indian War.**

At first, colonists did not seek independence from England. They wanted to have the same relationship with the crown that had existed before all the taxes. Like his father before him, John was elected to the Braintree town council, where he worked to eliminate the unfair taxes. In March of 1766, Parliament gave in to the colonists' outrage by repealing

This cartoon was published the day of the repeal, showing defeated supporters of the Stamp Act giving it a funeral.

the Stamp Act. The streets were filled with celebrating Americans. Feeling ill, Abigail remained at home to rest.

Boycotts in Boston

The celebration was short-lived. Parliament issued the Declaratory Act, stating that Great Britain could and would tax the colonists. The Townsend Revenue Acts that taxed glass, lead, paint, paper, and tea followed this. Even those colonists loyal to King George III felt these taxes were unfair. The Patriots—those who were willing to break from England over the issue of taxation without representation—smuggled merchandise into the colonies to avoid paying England's high taxes. To halt the smugglers, British warships closed Boston Harbor.

On July 11, 1767, Abigail gave birth to their son, John Quincy Adams. In the winter of 1768, Susanna was born. Susanna was never strong and died when she was 13 months old.

To reduce John's long commute and increase family time, Abigail and the children moved into the town of Boston. Their home was two blocks from the Massachusetts Assembly in the Old State House. There, Abigail

The Boston Massacre

could hear British soldiers drilling in the city streets. On March 5, 1770, colonists threw snowballs and insults at a British soldier who stood duty at his post. The soldier sent for help from his military unit. More colonists gathered, and British soldiers ordered them back. In an explosion of gunshots, 11 colonists were wounded. Five died from their wounds.

Patriots called the incident the Boston Massacre, and a trial was held. John defended the British soldiers in court. Bostonians wanted the eight soldiers hanged, but John's arguments won a non-guilty verdict for six. Two were convicted of manslaughter; their punishment was branding. The verdicts added to John's reputation as a fair and honest man.

On May 29, 1770, Abigail gave birth to Charles Adams. In 1772, Thomas Boylston joined their family. In 1778, John and Abigail's last baby, a girl named Elizabeth, was stillborn.

Revolution

Parliament was not finished taxing the colonies. In 1773, the Tea Act taxed New England's most popular drink. On December 16 of that year, Patriots protested the Tea Act. A group called the Sons of Liberty dressed like Mohawk Indians and tossed the cargo of tea from three ships into the sea. The event was called the Boston Tea Party.

The Boston Tea Party

England responded by limiting shipping and cargoes with the Coercive Acts. The colonists quickly renamed these the Intolerable Acts. When the British closed Boston's port, John and Abigail felt their family would be safer back at the farm in Braintree.

But John was not home for long. In the hot and humid August of 1774, Abigail packed clothes and food for his journey from Boston to Philadelphia. He would be a delegate to the first Continental Congress. The couple did not know how long they would be apart. Much as Abigail wanted John to be home with their growing family, she understood that her husband would make good decisions regarding the trouble between the colonies and Great Britain.

Representatives from all thirteen colonies gathered in Pennsylvania to discuss the Intolerable Acts. John wrote to Abigail, "This assembly is like no other that ever existed. Every man in it is a great man—an orator, a critic, a statesman . . ."[3]

With the port closed in Boston, many people were without work, including field hands, merchants, sailors, and shipbuilders. Resentment grew toward the British who occupied Boston. Other colonies objected to Great Britain's harsh treatment, which they knew could extend to them. In April 1775, British General Thomas Gage marched to Concord and Lexington to arrest revolutionary leaders John Hancock and John's cousin, Sam Adams. When the British regiment arrived at Concord and Lexington, Hancock and Sam Adams were gone. Instead, minutemen were ready and waiting. Shots were fired. The Revolutionary War had begun.

Shopping on the Black Market

When John traveled in the colonies and later to Europe, Abigail frequently included a shopping list in her letters to her husband. A frugal shopper, she knew which items had gone up in price and which were unavailable. Some items that John purchased and sent to Abigail were lost on the way, and others were damaged. During this time of scarcity for the residents of Massachusetts, Abigail often sold what she received and used the money to support the farm.

In her letters to John dated 1780, Abigail's shopping list included black satin for cloaks, black lace, calico, Irish linen, black silk gloves, wool for two winter gowns, shoe binding, a pound of white thread, and the best hyson tea.[4]

Abigail missed her husband dearly. In her letter of July 24, 1780, she wrote, "I have a request to you which I hope you will not disappoint me of, a miniature of him I best love."[5] Abigail wanted a picture of John to look at during his absence. Without the invention of photography, John would have to find a portrait painter to paint his likeness.

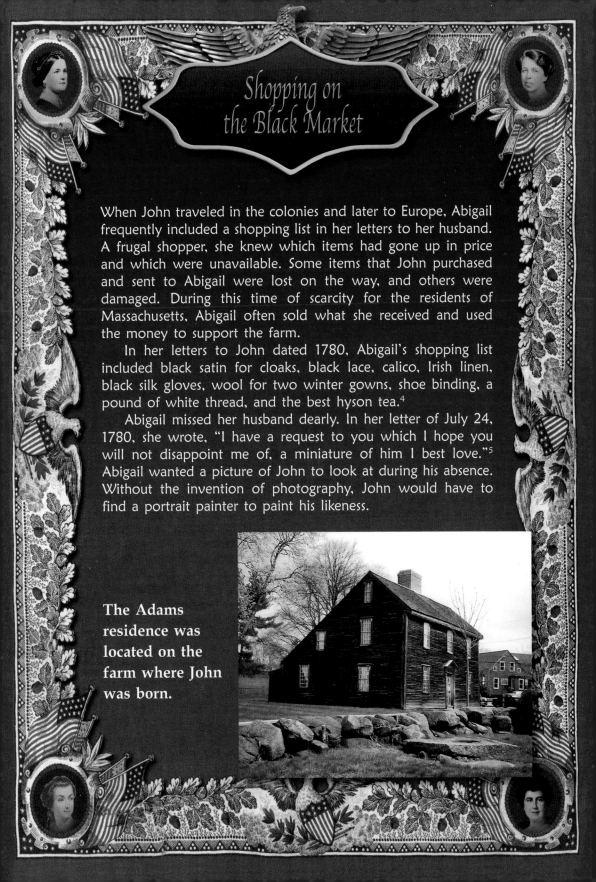

The Adams residence was located on the farm where John was born.

Chapter Three
LIBERTY FOR ALL

"Remember the Ladies, and be more generous and favourable to them than your ancestors. Do not put such unlimited power into the hands of the Husbands. Remember all Men would be tyrants if they could. If perticuliar [sic] care and attention is not paid to the Laidies [sic] we are determined to foment a Rebelion, [sic] and will not hold ourselves bound by any Laws in which we have no voice, or Representation."[1]

From Abigail to John
March 31, 1776

Abigail Adams stood on Penn's Hill and held the hand of her seven-year-old son, John Quincy. On the early morning of June 17, 1775, smoke filled their noses and stung their eyes as gusts of heat reached them on the hill. Abigail clutched young John close as the boy cried.

Crowded atop surrounding hills and rooftops, shocked residents watched British soldiers torching buildings as they marched through the small town of Charlestown at the base of Breed's Hill. Horrified, Abigail and

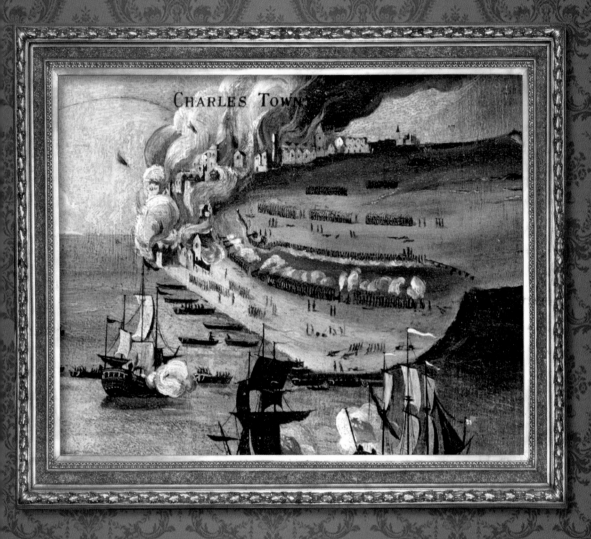

Marching through Charlestown, Massachusetts, the British set fire to the town. The torched buildings erupted into pyramids of fire that added to the rising heat of the June afternoon.

Abigail watched as the first bloody battle of the Revolutionary War was fought near their farm, lasting two hours and resulting in some 1,400 casualties.

young John saw the familiar church and storefronts erupt into flames. Then they watched the British climb the hill to attack the band of rebel soldiers.

The militia was an unorganized bunch of friends and neighbors arrayed to fight the highly trained British soldiers. The previous night, the Americans positioned themselves on the rise and rushed to construct protective breastworks of earth, fence posts, and stone.

The militia fired muskets at the British, who fired back with cannons. Abigail and John Quincy were grieved as friends and neighbors were wounded and killed. The Americans forced the British to withdraw twice but were routed on the third attack.

At the battle's end, over 1,000 British troops were dead and 400 American men had lost their lives in the fight called the Battle of Bunker Hill. Though the battle had been lost, the Americans celebrated. They had held off the powerful British army until the ammunition was gone. Now they knew the enemy could be stopped. Independence was possible.

This first true battle of the Revolutionary War was also the bloodiest. Young John Quincy, who would later become the sixth president of the United States, had observed firsthand the great price brave Americans paid for liberty. In a letter to her husband, Abigail wrote, "The Day; perhaps the decisive Day has come on which the fate of America depends."[2]

Remember the Ladies

Neither Abigail nor John thought that John's position as a delegate would keep him away from home so often, so long. During his absences over the next ten years, Abigail wisely managed the farm and the family's business matters.

Her days without her partner were exhausting. Determined to give her children a good education, she taught them at home. She also planted, harvested, and raised animals on the farm. She coordinated tenant farmers on their land; hired help for the tasks she could not do herself; preserved food for winter; made soap, candles, and cheese; and wove cloth for their clothing. She did all this while boycotting the highly taxed items from Europe, and without other common items that were unavailable after the seaport closed.

George Washington

At the second meeting of the Continental Congress, John recommended George Washington as commander of the Patriot army, now called the Continental Army. Abigail was in Cambridge, Massachusetts, when Washington took leadership of the new and untrained army. She wrote to John that Washington was a modest, gentleman soldier who exhibited "dignity with ease."

The Second Continental Congress appointed John Adams, Benjamin Franklin, and Thomas Jefferson to a five-member committee to write a declaration of independence.

John, Thomas Jefferson, and Benjamin Franklin stayed in Philadelphia to draft what would become the Declaration of Independence. John sent Abigail a persuasive pamphlet by Thomas Paine titled *Common Sense*. This powerful paper convinced many undecided Americans to fight for independence.

Abigail had never favored slavery and was passionate about females having the same opportunities for education as males. In 1797, she taught a young black boy to read and write, but a neighbor objected when Abigail sent the boy to evening school to learn to cipher. Abigail responded, "Merely because his Face is Black, is he to be denied instruction?"[3] She was well aware that while colonial men were fighting for their right to self-government, freedom for all did not extend to women and slaves.

In her letter to John on May 7, 1776, Abigail urged, "I can not say that I think you very generous to the Ladies, for whilst you are proclaiming peace and good will to Men, Emancipating all Nations, you insist upon retaining an absolute power over Wives. But you must remember that Arbitrary power is like most other things which are very hard, very liable to be broken — and . . . we have it in our power not only to free ourselves but to subdue our Masters, and without violence throw both your natural and legal authority at our feet."[4]

Pewter for Bullets

John wrote to Abigail that she must protect the children and run to the hills if the British army invaded. But when Abigail's neighbors streamed past her home on the road out of town as the British advanced, Abigail remained steadfast.

Travelers were surprised that Abigail and her children chose to remain on their farm. They were even more surprised that the lady of the house and her children fed them on their way. When the minutemen noticed her pewter serving pieces, Abigail gave these to the Patriots to be melted down for bullets.

The British invaded Philadelphia but found the town mostly deserted. John had gone home to his family, where he planned to continue farming and practicing law. But soon, Congress sent John to Europe to form an alliance with France. John wanted to take his family, but crossing the Atlantic in the winter with British warships patrolling the seas was too dangerous. Abigail packed food for her husband and ten-year-old John Quincy. The boy and his father set sail on February 14, 1778. Their trip

Young John Quincy Adams

was successful, and John and John Quincy returned home in 1779 in time to help Abigail with the harvest.

Mere months later, Abigail once again said good-bye to John. At the request of Congress, John traveled to Europe to begin peace negotiations. This time John Quincy and Charles went with him.

From 1775 to 1783, the Revolutionary War raged. Finally General George Washington, aided by the young Marquis de Lafayette, defeated British Lieutenant General Lord Charles Cornwallis in a decisive battle at Yorktown.

After nearly a decade of conflict, armistice was declared. On September 3, 1783, following extensive negotiations, American and British commissioners signed a treaty in Paris in which Great Britain officially agreed to peace. The Revolutionary War was over, and the United States became its own country.

American peace commissioners John Jay, John Adams, Benjamin Franklin, and Henry Laurens signed the preliminary articles of peace on November 30, 1782.

Charles was nine years old and John Quincy was twelve when they crossed the Atlantic with their father.

Abigail knew that John's work for the new nation was vital, but she could not help missing him and her sons when they were away. "Dearest of Friends," she wrote to John on November 14, 1779, "My table I sit down to it but cannot swallow my food. . . . My dear sons I cannot think of them without a tear, little do they know the feelings of a Mothers Heart! May they be good and usefull as their Father then they will in some measure reward the anxiety of a Mother. My tenderest love to them."[5]

The leaky ship, the *Sensible*, that carried John and their sons to Europe barely avoided sinking. With seven feet of water in its hold, the ship reached Spain. John and the boys had to make a rugged winter journey overland to Paris. John's letter to Abigail from Bilbao, Spain, on January 16, 1780, read, "I have undergone the greatest Anxiety for the Children, thro a tedious Journey and Voyage. I hope their Travels will be of Service to them, but those at home are best off."[6]

John comforted Abigail from Paris in a letter that spring: "Charles is as well beloved here as at home. Wherever he goes everybody loves him."[7]

Charles accompanied his father and brother to Europe. In December 1781, Charles returned to the United States. He graduated from Harvard Law School in 1789.

Chapter Four
SECOND FIRST LADY

"Patriotism in the female Sex is the most disinterested [unselfish] of all virtues. Excluded from honours and from offices, we cannot attach ourselves to the State or Government. . . . Even in the freest countrys our property is subject to the controul and disposal of our partners, to whom the Laws have given a soverign Authority. Deprived of a voice in Legislation, obliged to submit to those Laws which are imposed upon us, is it not sufficient to make us indifferent to the publick Welfare? Yet all History and every age exhibit Instances of patriotick virtue in the female Sex; which considering our situation equals the most Heroick of yours."[1]

To John Adams from Abigail Adams, June 17, 1782

It had been four years since Abigail saw her husband and son when she and Nabby sailed to Paris to join John at his diplomatic post. Thomas remained in Massachusetts with Abigail's sister. Aboard the *Active* in 1784, Abigail was certain the ship derived its name from the sickness induced by tossing and rolling on the ocean. Once the illness subsided, Abigail spent

Whether at home in Peacefield or in the capital, Abigail Adams used her influence and energy to promote education and equal opportunities for all.

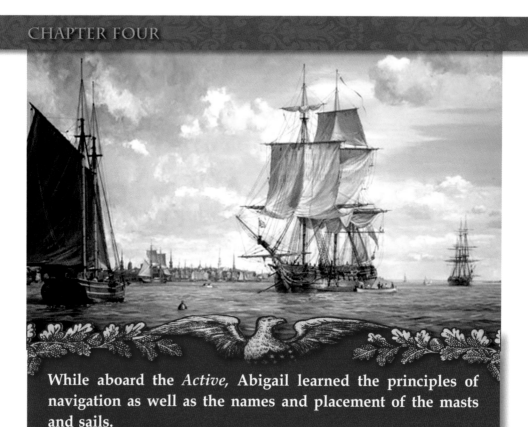

While aboard the *Active*, Abigail learned the principles of navigation as well as the names and placement of the masts and sails.

the miserable voyage teaching the cook how to properly prepare food, and she used plenty of vinegar to tidy the filthy vessel.

In France, Abigail and Nabby could hardly believe how tall and mature John Quincy had grown. As his father's assistant, John Quincy was now fluent in French. He had been present at the signing of the peace treaty, and he had traveled to Russia three times as secretary to envoy Francis Dana. For his entire life, John Quincy kept a diary of all his adventures. The massive collection of fifty journals became a valuable resource on the early years of the United States.

John broke away from his diplomatic work and came to meet his family. In France, at last John and Abigail were together again. At first, French customs seemed odd to Abigail, but she came to admire the theater and ballet. Dr. Benjamin Franklin was at the center of French society. Abigail met Thomas Jefferson and she occasionally wrote letters to Jefferson regarding politics.

The following year, Abigail and John moved to England, where John took his post as ambassador of the United States to his former king. Having just lost the colonial war, King George III and Queen Charlotte were not cordial to Abigail. John and Abigail were relieved when John's time as America's diplomat ended in 1788 and he was recalled home.

While in London, John purchased a 40-acre farm in Quincy for 600 English pounds. The couple returned to the United States to their new gentleman's farm, which they named Peacefield. Having lived in fancy homes in Europe, the smaller Peacefield, built in 1731, felt to Abigail like a "wren's nest."[2]

When John and Abigail purchased Peacefield, the house had only two small rooms, two bedrooms, and an attic. Additions were built over many decades.

Nearly the same age as John Adams, George Washington was unanimously elected president of the new nation. In 1789, John Adams was elected vice president. He was sworn into office before George Washington. Abigail settled things at the farm and joined her husband at the capital, which at the time was in New York.

Both the President and Vice President were responsible for finding their own places to live. Though John and Abigail preferred something modest, they rented rooms to reflect the position of the nation's second highest office. Many society ladies came to call, but Abigail considered endless visits a waste of time. The ladies left their calling cards. To be polite, Abigail returned the visits, but she left her cards in the evening when she knew they would be busy at social events.

One visitor Abigail welcomed was First Lady Martha Washington. Having learned court etiquette while in Europe as an ambassador's wife, Abigail assisted First Lady Martha Washington in hosting visitors from abroad. The two women recognized their unique position of influence. Martha was friendly in social settings. Abigail often worried that her own knack for speaking her mind would offend others. Later, when Abigail became First Lady, Martha sent venison and other foods from Mount Vernon to help Abigail feed guests at the White House. When John's presidency ended, the one person Abigail visited before retiring to Peacefield was Martha.

President John Adams

After his second term as President, George Washington declined to run for a third term. Abigail was at Peacefield during John's election and inauguration as President. She had experienced debilitating illness again and was recovering in Braintree.

John wrote to Abigail, "I never wanted your Advice and assistance more in my life." Later he wrote, "The Times are critical and dangerous, and I must have you here to assist me."[3]

For the four years of John's presidency, Abigail was with him for only eighteen months. John and Abigail rented the same home that George and Martha Washington had occupied. They were dismayed to find that the large home needed expensive repairs. Though John received a salary, it was not enough to pay for the rental and upkeep of the home, nor the entertaining necessary for the position of the President. Soon they were in debt.

The next temporary capital was in Philadelphia. For four months, John and Abigail lived there. Then, in 1800, for the final months of John's presidency, they moved into the newly constructed White House in Washington, D.C. They were the first president and First Lady to live in the new mansion.

Abigail found the cold, damp house to be dismal. Although their furniture had been moved in, the house wasn't completely finished. Water had to be carried from a park five blocks away, and she had to hang her laundry to dry in the East Room. Despite the hardship, Abigail hosted

The first First Lady to live in the White House, Abigail referred to the presidential residence as the great castle.

Monday night public receptions and Wednesday night formal dinners for members of Congress. She also organized a Fourth of July celebration.

Just a few weeks after she arrived in Washington, Abigail received devastating news. Her son Charles had died of alcoholism. He left behind his wife, Sally Smith, and daughters, Susanna Boylston and Louisa Abigail.

John Adams campaigned for a second term as president but lost to Thomas Jefferson, who had undermined John's administration. Abigail had approved of John's work to pass the Alien and Sedition Acts. These laws censored the press and restricted access for immigrants who wanted to become U.S. citizens. They also declared noncitizens living in the United States to be enemies in time of war. Jefferson spoke out against these acts and soundly defeated his former friend for the presidency.

Abigail recalled the years she had written letters and discussed political matters with Jefferson. She was the one Jefferson had chosen to raise his daughter when his wife died. For John and Abigail, Jefferson's actions felt like a betrayal of their friendship.

In February of 1801, Abigail and John left the White House and retired from public life to their beloved farm in Quincy, Massachusetts. For the first time in 36 years of marriage, John and Abigail were not separated for the sake of politics. At last, their correspondence was no longer necessary. They were no longer apart.

Fellow Founding Father Thomas Jefferson was sworn in as the third President on March 4, 1801.

Life in Europe was far different from what Abigail had experienced growing up in Massachusetts and living on the farm. Taking in European culture, Abigail loved the work of Handel, who composed *The Messiah*. She was not a fan of Shakespeare, nor did she initially like the ballet, where the ballerinas danced "showing their garters and drawers, as though no petticoats had been worn"[4]

After four years apart, being reunited as a family was the highlight. In her journal, Nabby described returning to their apartments to find her father's hat and two books on the table. "Up I flew, to his chamber, where he was lying down, he raised himself upon my knocking softly at the door, and received me with all the tenderness of an affectionate parent after so long an absence. Sure I am, I never felt more agitation of spirits in my life; it will not do to describe."[5]

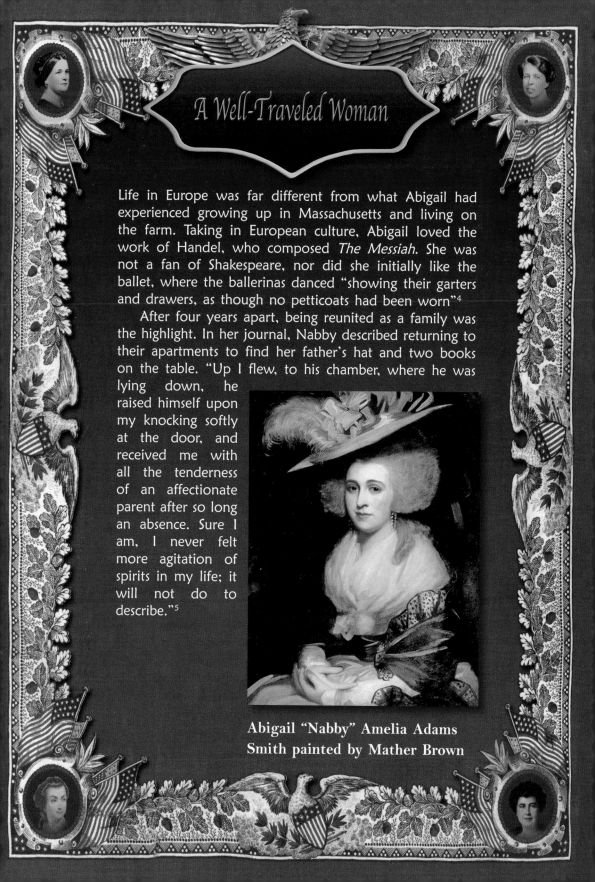

Abigail "Nabby" Amelia Adams Smith painted by Mather Brown

Chapter Five
MRS. PRESIDENT?

"I dare say, there is not a lady in America treated with a more curious dish of politics than is contained in the enclosed papers . . . by no means let them go out of your hands."[1]

John Adams to Abigail, Paris, December 28, 1782

After John's presidency, Abigail added a wing to Peacefield that doubled the size of the home. For nearly two decades, she and John enjoyed retired life together there. Abigail wrote to Jefferson and renewed old friendships. John and Abigail read books, discussed politics, raised an orchard and crops, and hosted their children and grandchildren.

In 1813 Nabby became seriously ill. She traveled from New York to be home at Peacefield, where she died of breast cancer at age 48.

Five years later, typhoid fever swept the area. Abigail's health was already fragile, and she died on October 28, 1818, two weeks short of her 74th birthday. Her last words were, "Do not grieve, my friend, my dearest friend. I am ready to go. And John, it will not be long."[2]

The wife of one president and mother of another, Abigail defined the role of First Lady by her patriotism, gracious formality, and devotion to her family.

When John died on July 4, 1826, he was buried beside his dearest friend. Their crypt is in the United First Parish Church, also called Church of the Presidents, in John's hometown of Quincy.[3]

Abigail Smith Adams was one of the most influential women of the American Revolutionary period. Because her husband valued her keen observations, some politicians called her Mrs. President. In an age when Patriots insisted on representation—a voice—in Great Britain's Parliament, Abigail Adams made it possible for women to eventually have a voice in American government. Abigail demonstrated the value of educated women. She spoke her mind so that others could support causes they felt were important.

Abigail's Legacy

As the mother of five, Abigail schooled her children, managed the family farm and finances, and encouraged her husband in the cause of liberty. Willingly, she boycotted Great Britain's overpriced supplies, doing without and substituting where she could. Her home was a refuge for neighbors, colonists, and militia who needed food and shelter. She generously held nothing back, including her pewter when minutemen required musket balls. Abigail went where she was needed, from farm to city to Europe and

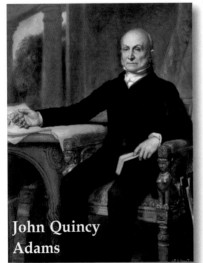

John Quincy
Adams

to the White House, to help the cause of liberty and the founding of the United States.

Abigail's childhood home in Weymouth survived two relocations and is preserved as a national monument. In Quincy, Peacefield remained home for four generations of the Adams descendants. After John and Abigail, it passed to President John Quincy Adams, then to Civil War Minister to Great Britain, Charles Francis Adams. Until 1927, it remained with literary historians Henry and Brooks Adams.

Built in 1873, the Stone Library is adjacent to the Adams residence in Peacefield and houses the family's rare and heirloom books.

The home where John Adams was born is 75 feet from the matching saltbox house where Abigail later gave birth to their daughter and the sixth U.S. President John Quincy Adams. The two homes are the oldest preserved presidential birthplaces. At the historic site of Peacefield is a large fireproof library. John Quincy left the family book collection to his son, Charles Francis. According to his father's wishes, Charles built the Stone Library to house the family's 12,000 volumes, including the original 1,200 books that had belonged to Abigail and John. In this stately building, Charles compiled *The Letters of Abigail Adams*.

Woman of Influence

By boldly thinking for herself and sharing her opinions about government and politics, Abigail contributed to the decisions made by delegates, representatives, and presidents. In an age when women had limited opportunities, Abigail championed freedom for all. Spanning dozens of years, the more than 1,100 surviving letters of Abigail and John gave the world an accurate account of the courageous people who invested their time, talent, and treasure into the Great American Experiment.

Abigail schooled her children and passed down a deep appreciation books, life-long learning, and civic responsibility.

As wife and mother, Abigail showed extraordinary stewardship, courage, and resourcefulness in keeping home and family functioning. Her patience, creativity, and industry allowed John to focus on the founding of the United States. Abigail was a devoted partner and confidante to her husband, who valued her input on matters of home and state. For John, who was often self-conscious, Abigail was a stabilizing and encouraging wife. Theirs was a marriage of soul mates.

Abigail did not allow social limitations to hold her back. She proved that educated women could be excellent wives, mothers, and contributing members of society. Her eagerness to engage in culture and politics was a powerful support for her husband and a strong foundation for her son, John Quincy. Abigail never saw her son become the sixth president of the United States. She died before John Quincy's election, but she was proud of his work as an international diplomat. Upon his mother's death in 1818, John Quincy wrote that Abigail displayed all the excellent qualities a woman could have.

Abigail's Legacy

Abigail's influence as a mother continued to impact history long after her death. As a parent she loved their father, taught her children, and encouraged them in their own future. During the four years John Quincy was in Europe with his father, Abigail continued to guide his development.

In her letter to John Quincy dated January 19, 1780, she wrote, "War, Tyranny and Desolation are the Scourges of the Almighty, and ought no doubt to be deprecated. Yet is your Lot my Son to be an Eye witness of these Calimities in your own Native Land, and at the same time to owe your existence among a people who have made a glorious defence of their invaded Liberties, and who, aided by generous and powerfull Ally, with the blessing of heaven will transmit this inheritance to ages yet unborn."[4] Indeed, the United States continues to enjoy this inheritance.

Born to parents who encouraged her desire to learn, Abigail Adams was perhaps the most influential woman of her time.

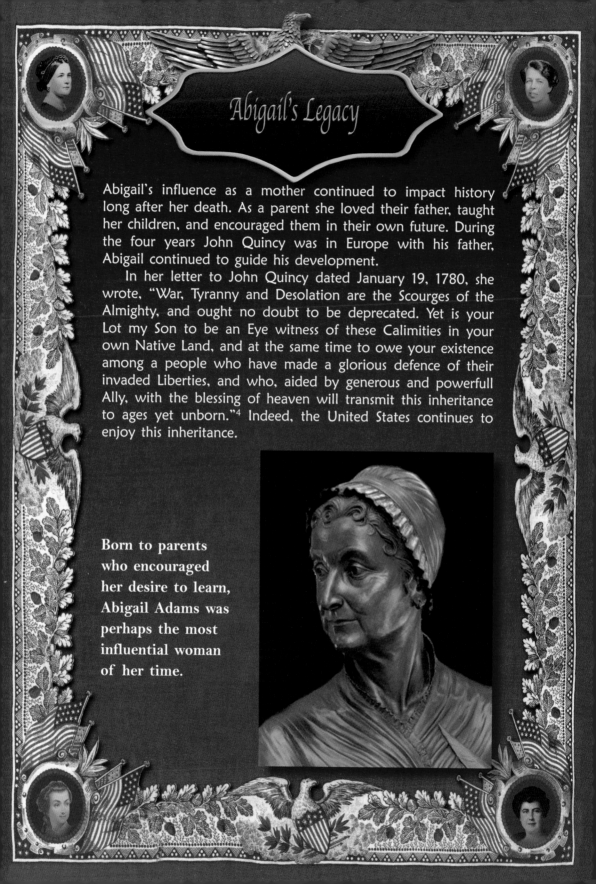

1744   Abigail Smith is born to the Reverend William Smith and Elizabeth Quincy Smith.

1764   On October 25, future President John Adams and Abigail Smith marry.

1765   Daughter Abigail (Nabby) Adams is born.

1767   Son John Quincy Adams, future sixth president of the United States, is born.

1768   Daughter Susanna Adams is born.

1770   Daughter Susanna Adams dies at 13 months old. Son Charles Adams is born.

1772   Son Thomas Boylston Adams is born.

1774   John Adams represents Massachusetts at the First Continental Congress.

1775   Abigail and John Quincy witness the Battle of Bunker Hill, the first and bloodiest battle of the Revolutionary War.

1776   John Adams helps write the Declaration of Independence, and the colonists declare their independence from England.

1783   Abigail and Nabby join John and John Quincy in Europe after John Adams signs Treaty of Paris. The treaty ends the Revolutionary War.

1788   Abigail goes to New York when John is elected the first vice president of the United States.

1793   John is reelected vice president and returns to Philadelphia; Abigail remains in Quincy.

1796   When John takes office as president, Abigail becomes the second First Lady of the United States.

1800   Abigail and John are the first family to live in the White House.

1801   Abigail and John retire to Quincy.

1813   Abigail's daughter, Nabby, dies of breast cancer.

1818   Abigail Smith Adams dies from typhoid fever.

1825   John Quincy Adams takes office as the sixth president of the United States.

1826   Abigail's husband, John Adams, dies in Quincy on July 4, fifty years after the Declaration of Independence was signed. Thomas Jefferson dies the same day.

Chapter 1. Dame School

1. Edited by L.H. Butterfield, Marc Friedlaender, Mary-Jo Kline, *The Book of Abigail and John; Selected Letters of the Adams Family 1762-1784* (Cambridge, Massachusetts: Harvard University Press), p. 153.
2. "First Lady Biography: Abigail Smith Adams," The National First Ladies' Library, http://www.firstladies.org/biographies/firstladies.aspx?biography=2. Accessed May, 2015
3. David McCullough, *John Adams* (New York: Simon and Schuster, 2001), p. 19.
4. Ibid, p. 8
5. "Adams National Historic Park," National Park Service, accessed June 14, 2015, http://www.nps.gov/adam/learn/historyculture/abigail-adams-1744-1818.htm

Chapter 2. Taxes and Tension

1. David McCullough, *John Adams* (New York: Simon and Schuster, 2001), preface.
2. Ibid., p. 61.
3. McCullough, p. 86.
4. Edited by L.H. Butterfield, Marc Friedlaender, Mary-Jo Kline, *The Book of Abigail and John; Selected Letters of the Adams Family 1762–1784* (Cambridge, Massachusetts, Harvard University Press), pp. 263–264.
5. Ibid., p. 265.

Chapter 3. Liberty for All

1. Edited by L.H. Butterfield, Marc Friedlaender, Mary-Jo Kline, *The Book of Abigail and John; Selected Letters of the Adams Family 1762-1784* (Cambridge, Massachusetts: Harvard University Press), p. 121.
2. Ibid, p. 90.
3. "First Lady Biography: Abigail Smith Adams," The National First Ladies' Library, accessed June 14, 2015, http://www.firstladies.org/curriculum/educational-biography.aspx?biography=2
4. Butterfield, Friedlaender, and Kline, p. 127.
5. Ibid., p. 245.
6. Ibid., p. 251.
7. Ibid., p. 256.
8. Ibid., p. 261.

Chapter 4. Second First Lady

1. Abigail Adams Historical Society, Abigail's Letters
   http://www.abigailadamsbirthplace.com/letters/

2. Hugh Howard, "Revolutionary Real Estate," Smithsonian, December 2007,
   http://www.smithsonianmag.com/history/revolutionary-real-estate-180075828/?c=y&page=2

3. "First Lady Biography: Abigail Smith Adams," The National First Ladies' Library,
   http://www.firstladies.org/biographies/firstladies.aspx?biography=2http://www.firstladies.org/biographies/firstladies.aspx?biography=2, accessed May, 2015

4. Carl Sferrazza Anthony, First Ladies: The Saga of the Presidents' Wives and Their Power 1789-1961 (New York, Quill William Morrow, 1990) p. 61

5. Edited by L.H. Butterfield, Marc Friedlaender, Mary-Jo Kline, *The Book of Abigail and John; Selected Letters of the Adams Family 1762-1784* (Cambridge, Massachusetts, Harvard University Press) p. 398.

Chapter 5. Mrs. President?

1. Carl Sferrazza Anthony, First Ladies: The Saga of the Presidents' Wives and Their Power 1789-1961 (New York, Quill William Morrow, 1990) p. 61.

2. American History Central, "AbigailAdams," http://www.americanhistorycentral.com/entry.php?rec=460

3. "John Quincy Adams Grieves for His Mother, Abigail Adams," New England Historical Society. http://www.newenglandhistoricalsociety.com/john-quincy-adams-grieves-mother-abigail-adams/

4. Margaret Brown Klapthor, *The First Ladies,* (The White House Historical Association and National Geographic Society, 1999) p. 11.

5. Edited by L.H. Butterfield, Marc Friedlaender, Mary-Jo Kline, *The Book of Abigail and John; Selected Letters of the Adams Family 1762-1784* (Cambridge, Massachusetts, Harvard University Press) p. 253.

Books

Kelley, True. *Who Was Abigail Adams?* New York: Grosset & Dunlap, 2014.

Schwartz Foster, Feather. *The First Ladies: From Martha Washington to Mamie Eisenhower, An Intimate Portrait of the Women Who Shaped America,* Napersville, Illinois: Cumberland House, 2011.

Somervill, Barbara A. *Abigail Adams: Courageous Patriot and First Lady.* Minneapolis: Compass Point Books, 2006.

Wagoner, Jean Brown. *Abigail Adams: Girl of Colonial Days.* New York: Simon & Schuster, 2008.

Works Consulted

Adams, John, and Charles Francis Adams. John Adams Autobiography. Amazon Digital, 2011.

Angelo, Bonnie. *First Mothers: The Women Who Shaped the Presidents.* New York: Harper Collins, 2000.

Anthony, Carl Sferranzza. *First Ladies: The Saga of the Presidents' Wives and Their Power, 1789–1961.* New York: William Morrow and Company, Inc., 1990.

Butterfield, L.H., Marc Friedlaender, and Mary-Jo Kline. *The Book of Abigail and John: Selected Letters of the Adams Family 1762–1784.* Cambridge: Harvard University Press, 2002.

Diane Jacobs, *Dear Abigail* (New York, Ballantine Books, 2014)

Holton, Woody. *Abigail Adams.* New York: Atria Publishing, 2010.

Klapthor, Margaret Brown. *The First Ladies.* Washington, D.C.: White House Historical Association with the cooperation of the National Geographic Society, 1999.

McCullough, David. *John Adams.* New York: Simon and Schuster, 2002.

On the Internet

The Abigail Adams Birthplace
http://AbigailAdamsBirthplace.com

Adams National Historical Park
http://www.nps.gov/adam/learn/historyculture/places.htm

National First Ladies' Libraries: Abigail Adams
http://www.firstladies.org/biographies/firstladies.aspx?biography=29

The Smithsonian: The True Story of the Battle of Bunker Hill
http://www.smithsonianmag.com/history/the-true-story-of-the-battle-of-bunker-hill-36721984/?no-ist=&page=1

This Day in History: Abigail Adams
http://www.history.com/search?q=Abigail%20Adams

administration (ad-mih-nih-STRAY-shun)—The government officials who work under a president.

arbitrary (AR-bih-trayr-ee)—Chosen without weighing the facts.

armistice (ARH-mi-stis)—An agreement between sides to stop fighting and discuss peace terms.

boycott (BOY-kot)—To express disapproval by refusing to buy things from a company or a country.

campaign (kam-PAYN)—A series of speeches, meetings, advertisements, and other actions done in order to win votes.

candidate (KAN-dih-dayt)—A person who is running for a position or for political office.

cipher (SY-fur)—To write; to do math.

confidante (KON-fee-dahnt)—A person another trusts with secret and private information.

courtship (KOHRT-ship)—The dating period before marriage.

debilitating (deh-BIL-ih-tay-ting)—Causing weakness or death.

delegate (DEL-ih-git)—A person who represents and speaks for others.

descendant (dih-SEN-dunt)—A person's child or later offspring.

emancipating (ee-MAN-sih-pay-ting)—Setting free from legal, social, or political bonds.

envoy (ON-voy)—A representative sent by one government to another, similar to an ambassador but usually with less power.

inauguration (in-aw-gyuh-RAY-shun)—A ceremony to install a person into office.

legacy (LEH-guh-see)—Property or ideas received from someone who has died.

militia (mil-IH-shuh)—A group of citizen soldiers called out only in an emergency.

minutemen (MIN-it-men)—American citizen soldiers during the Revolutionary War who were ready for service at a "minute's" notice.

pewter (PYOO-ter)—A type of metal that includes mostly tin, some lead, and trace copper and antimony; it was often used for making plates and cups.

politics (PAH-lih-tiks)—Meetings and strategies involved in running a government.

retaliate (ree-TAL-ee-ayt)—To get back at someone, usually through a counterattack.

revolution (rev-uh-LOO-shun)—An overthrow of a government by the people governed.

saltbox (SALT-boks)—A Colonial home with two stories in front and one story in back, and a gable roof that extends over the rear.

stewardship (STOO-werd-ship)—The responsibility of protecting something.

undermine (UN-der-myn)—To purposely weaken someone else's position or authority.

PeggySue Wells is the bestselling and award-winning author of two dozen books, including a *USA Today* and *Wall Street Journal* bestseller and audio finalist. Her titles are published nationally and internationally and have been translated into several languages. Radio cohost and mother of seven children, PeggySue visits schools to share with students the secrets that make reading and writing fun. Visit www.PeggySueWells.com.